OUR ETERNAL RELATIONSHIP

10 Contemplations for a Connected Life

JOSEPH V. McCARTHY

Copyright © 2021 Joseph V. McCarthy

ISBN: 978-1-922565-32-7
Published by Vivid Publishing
A division of Fontaine Publishing Group
P.O. Box 948, Fremantle
Western Australia 6959
www.vividpublishing.com.au

A catalogue record for this
book is available from the
National Library of Australia

NATIONAL
LIBRARY
OF AUSTRALIA

THE EMBRACE

At some point in our lives, we are exposed to spiritual insights that prompt us to pause what we are doing, and question our place in the world. The insights might be personal experiences, breathtaking landscapes, or even reading a passage in a book for the first time. For many people, these insights have little relevance to their day-to-day lives, and before long they forget. For others, these insights present another stepping stone on their spiritual journey, treasured for reflection upon, over and over. But for some people, the insight can be so transformative that their lives change completely, and for years they struggle with this piece of knowledge as it shatters the world perspective they once accepted without question. It was an insight such as this that thoroughly altered my view of the world, and which continues even today to influence my choices and life decisions.

When I was thirty-three, I received a spiritual experience. It began as a dream, then progressed into my waking consciousness. It was the catalyst for a journey that led me thousands of kilometres away from home, to live with strangers in an environment far removed from what I had known. Fifteen years later, I received two more experiences relevant to the first. Each of these three experiences confirmed the pathway on which I walked was the right one and gave me a sense of where I was headed next on my spiritual journey.

It has been twenty years since that first dream, and these spiritual experiences still affect me in everything I do. Although I have rarely shared my dreams with anyone, in the last few years I felt the call to relate my experiences, how they changed my life, and to share what I feel they mean for others. I have done this in the form of contemplations. In this introduction, I relate the spiritual experiences and how they affected my personal life.

I encourage you to ponder the meaning of the dreams and imagine how you might respond, in the hope my experiences may benefit you as well as me.

In the first dream, I found myself walking up the timber stairs of a monastery. I reached the top of the stairs and continued along a balcony. I had only walked a few steps when before me appeared a magnificent spiritual being, every part of her shining with light. The light was so brilliant I could not make out any of her features. She led me to an opening on the balcony, and I stood there, on the edge, preparing to step out into an unknown future. I was so nervous about falling into nothingness that I froze. The shining woman stood behind me now, and though I could not hear her voice, I sensed her assuring me that everything would be fine.

She then *embraced* me, and it was as if my mind went meta-nova.

No experience on Earth can compare to the power and energy that exploded through my being. I can only describe that feeling as the most sublime happiness. I saw light all around me, and it was shining out from inside me. I don't recall any thoughts of my own or from the woman. Welling up through this feeling was beautiful, beautiful gratitude; these words cannot do justice to what I was feeling. The exhilaration and relief were so great, I felt these feelings transform into the most pure, powerful energy I have ever known. I cannot imagine how anything in this universe could generate this most exquisite feeling.

After what may have been only minutes, the light dissipated, and I became conscious of lying in my bed in a dark room. I was as clear-headed as ever I have been in my life, but I could not move. The energy flowing through my body was still so powerful that I thought it could raise me a hundred metres into the air if I so wished. I felt as if every living creature for kilometres around would feel what was happening to me. I lay like this for at least fifteen minutes and, although it was after midnight, I could hear a bird singing just outside my bedroom window. When I was able to switch on the bedside light and sit up, I wrote down everything. I decided that night to do whatever I could to recover that wonderful, powerful feeling and to discover its meaning and purpose. I had no idea if it was a supernatural revelation or some kind of intellectual enlightenment, and I didn't really care. My desire to recapture that feeling was so strong that within days I had decided nothing else was as important. I was going to leave everything I was doing and pursue the spiritual and philosophical questions this experience presented to me.

At this time, I was working in a maximum-security prison. I co-ordinated the Sentence Management Unit, which gathered information about inmates to determine their security classification and management of their sentences. Before this I worked many years as a prison officer in the maximum, medium and low security divisions, and I was familiar with most of the officers and inmates of this large correctional complex. I felt comfortable in this environment and was very career driven. As a five-year plan, my goal was to attain the position of General Manager. But after that stunning spiritual experience, those career goals dissipated like smoke. All I could think of was somehow regaining the feeling of that embrace.

As a correctional officer, I was exposed to a very different perspective on life than I had known growing up in a large, supportive family with a morally formative education. In particular, working in the Sentence Management Unit gave me access to all the inmates' files, full of criminal histories, psychological reports, and judges' court remarks. These painted a picture of family environments and influences vastly different from those to which I had been exposed. The sons and daughters of career criminals had not been given the opportunities offered me, and their chances of a positive future, free from the influence of crime and substance abuse, were slim.

I had always been an avid reader of spiritual and philosophical books, and I enjoyed the insights they provided and the stability these ideas promoted in my daily life. But why should I be so lucky to have the inclination and education to be able to comprehend those insights when these people, domiciled in the prison, lived in despair and in an environment of fear and aggression? Many were caught in a cycle of imprisonment: re-entry into difficult life situations with poor coping skills, turning back to crime to make ends meet, and then their inevitable return to the misery of prison. It didn't seem fair to me that a deity would make a spiritual journey so easy for some and so hard for others. This was a question I wrestled with for a long time.

Working in a prison can have a detrimental effect on one's life, and the first few years in that environment I found myself becoming more cynical and critical. After my marriage broke down, as I endured the day-to-day challenges of prison life, I decided to reverse these negative changes in myself and work to return to my original, brighter nature and outlook on life. One of the methods I used for this was meditation, and this exposed me to the writings of monks and the virtues of monasticism. I was attracted to the idea of meditating to distance the world's day-to-day distractions and so concentrate more deeply on the great philosophical questions.

At a deeper level, in monastic thought, there was the practice of looking beyond the world in the pursuit of a perfect loving relationship with God. This contemplative focus resonated deeply within me. I had spent many years dealing with the disappointment of my failed marriage, and then recovering from this difficult period by reflecting on both good and bad times. I came to understand that a relationship requiring such depth of commitment initiates you into intimacy that enters the spiritual, whether you are aware of it or not. As in all intimate personal relationships, however long they last, experiencing this special union is something sacred that can never be taken away from you. An expression of mutual love can be treasured like a crystal of clarity, and can light your spiritual journey when the way in the world isn't so clear.

Recognising the value of relationships that enter the spiritual, I saw engagement in a monastic life as the allegory for a perfect marriage – all distractions placed to the side and complete attention focused on the object of my love. No matter how the relationship might falter, whatever unseen obstacles might arise, all thought and action would be to this end. It invited a commitment I respected and aspired to, but, although I was inspired by these ideas, at that time I had no desire to leave my situation and engage in a life of self-sacrifice, hidden away from the rest of the world. That was until I felt that spiritual embrace of a woman shining with light.

In the days following my experience, I had many questions as to what it all meant. I felt an affinity with this shining woman, as if I had always known her. Who was she? Why was she standing on the balcony of a religious institution? I needed time and freedom to find the answers, and I eventually decided I had to let go of everything I was doing and pursue the meaning of this experience as best I could. As I write this, I realise how impulsive I might appear, but it is a measure of how powerful and awe-inspiring my experience had been.

I desperately wanted to somehow reverse-engineer the feeling of that experience and share it with everyone. As the dream involved a monastery, I hoped this was a clue to guide me on my journey, and so I decided to become a monk. Within a year I found a monastery that accepted me, and, after nine years working in the prison system and thirty years living in North Queensland, I left for a monastic life at an abbey in Tarrawarra, Victoria, two-and-a-half thousand kilometres away.

Tarrawarra Abbey is a small community of contemplative monks whose spirituality is based on simplicity, obedience and mutual love. It is an enclosed community where monks stay within the monastery, and their work and lives revolve around communal prayer seven times a day. Many of the older monks came from Roscrea Abbey in Ireland, and there were others from Singapore, Tonga, Sri Lanka and Malaysia.

Despite coming from so many backgrounds and cultures, these men live together as a loving community of selfless people who gave up all they had in order to pray with each other for the world. There is a strong emphasis on reading and study too, and I remember these times as some of the happiest years of my life. I lived in the monastery for six years, worked in the dairy, learnt to play the pipe-organ, and at times sang as cantor in the choir.

During this time, I came into contact with *A Course in Miracles*, three books written by Helen Schucman, and they struck a deep chord within me. Simply put, the course suggests that we live in a world shining with divinity, but in order to see it we must learn to ignore our ego, which is successfully convincing us otherwise. The more I delved into the different spiritual perspective presented by these books, the more desperate I became to share with others the light burning within me.

I attempted to discuss this alternative perspective with other monks, but there was little interest to explore outside their tradition. I eventually found a responsive ear in a woman employed as a cook in our kitchen. She too was reading these books, and, over time and many discussions, we developed a closer relationship. It came time to make my final vows. However, after enduring a painful personal crisis during which I needed spiritual and emotional support not available in the monastery, I decided to leave and be with her, to discover anew the world outside, shining with the spirit.

Our relationship deepened and I lived with her in nearby Healesville. I found work as a bus driver and joined the State Emergency Services as a volunteer. Together my partner and I travelled around Europe and Australia whenever we could. We finished renovating her house, then we owner-built another house, also in Healesville. All through this time, I continued to seek understanding of my earlier spiritual experience. I also attempted to apply to my life all I had learnt as a contemplative monk and from *A Course in Miracles*, in a hectic and rapidly developing technological society. As much as I tried, I could not recover that powerful feeling of perfect happiness I felt during my original experience. I was plagued with doubts, wondering if the path I followed was just a foolish response to a dream far removed from the reality of this world.

Eventually, I became a training officer for emergency services in our district, which absorbed much of my spare time. Healesville is an attractive town at the foot of high mountains, featuring forests of mountain ash and tall tree ferns. The steady influx of tourists, sightseeing and visiting local wineries, meant there was also a high incidence of accidents. As emergency service workers, we were responsible for lost person searches, flood rescue, and car crash rescue. I witnessed many instances of survival and misfortune, and these opened my eyes to the fragility of this precious life most of us take so much for granted.

On one occasion I attended a crash and entrapment, with the car on its side and its roof removed. I crawled into the dashboard area and knelt over a deceased person in order to cut free someone hanging above who was barely alive. There were many other emergency workers involved, and it was a scene of frenzied activity and noise. During this rescue I felt a palpable sense of connection emanating from the deceased person below me, almost as if I were being acknowledged. From previous experiences of months of flashbacks after these accidents, I did my best not to look at the damaged body of the deceased. And yet, I definitely felt that this person somehow continued to relate to me, and I reflected on this long after the day of the rescue.

Searching for the deeper meaning of the connection I felt with this poor victim introduced me to the concept of near-death experiences, and I read many books on the subject. I discovered modern scientific research examining the possibility of our consciousness continuing after life in this world is over. An example is the book *Evidence of the Afterlife* by Jeffry Long MD with Paul Perry, a study collecting the near-death experiences of thousands of people from across the globe, from different cultures and faiths.

There were twelve elements common in many of these near-death experiences, which were shared by participants in the study. They included out-of-body experiences, heightened senses, intense positive emotions, passing through a tunnel, encountering supernatural light, meeting familiar beings, alterations of time and space, and a life review. What interested me most, however, was the intense positive emotions these people felt upon entering the after-life. The experiences shared by these thousands of subjects matched perfectly how I felt during my first spiritual experience.

It was around this time, probably ten years after I left the monastery, that I had my second spiritual encounter. This time, late at night, I lay in bed, drifting off to sleep. I dreamt I was at a village drinking-well, not in person, but as an observer. People from all corners of the world came to drink at this well, but it wasn't water they drank. It was peace, love and joy. I could sense these three feelings flowing from the well, and this was what the people sought. Immediately I was filled with the same immense happiness of my first dream, with all its power and energy. I jolted awake and the feeling diminished quickly.

When I got over my shock, I thought again about this well of peace, love and joy. Even though I was fully awake, again the power of that feeling returned as strong as ever. I instantly stopped myself thinking of it because it was so unbelievably intense. It had the strength and brilliance of the sun, and my mind could not bear it. I wanted it so much, but it was too overwhelming. I didn't want to disturb my partner as she was sound asleep, and so I lay there, elated that perhaps I could now turn on this feeling of energy whenever I wanted. Somehow, I managed to go back to sleep.

Next morning, I awoke and tried unsuccessfully to return to that state. I was very disappointed, but, as I reflected on the second experience, I felt that receiving this dream indicated I was still on the right spiritual path. It also affirmed for me the importance of all three qualities – peace, love and joy – for reaching the state of sublime happiness I sought. I believe anyone who experiences this state would also search wholeheartedly for these feelings. I eventually came to understand such experiences as spiritual awakenings. They are relevant to everyone alive, passed away or yet to come, and to everything that has a spirit. This new perspective changed my life completely.

I began researching and reflecting on everything I had learnt about peace, love and joy from the perspective of spirit. At the same time, my partner and I decided to sell our house and go our separate ways. Although the separation was amicable, it was nevertheless an unhappy period in my life, and I needed time to recover.

I moved into a small house, nestled in the forest outside Healesville, in a quiet area with lovely neighbours. Being single and without commitments, I entered a serene existence, conducive to meditation and reflection. Before long I was able to reach and sustain the sublime state of those spiritual awakenings, though not with the same intensity.

There was an aspect of our spiritual journey I constantly reflected on but struggled to understand. What is our relationship to one another from a spiritual perspective? Were we really billions of different individuals on our own journeys? Were we branches of the one tree? Were we each an awareness of one supreme being, like facets of a diamond?

It was after a year in this new house that I received the third experience. It was night and again I was on the verge of going to sleep. I felt myself rise and turn, and then I found myself looking down upon an immense group of beings. All creation was here, but they weren't physical. It was their affection I could sense or feel, and I can't describe how I knew this. None of them seemed immediately familiar, but I felt close to all of them. Everyone I could see was focused on each other, and they were all in love. Everyone's spirits were gathered together, and I could feel their unity, their pure love for each other.

I felt this in-loveness was the perfect expression of heaven. It wasn't a place or a time. This realm was the recognition and acceptance of *spiritual reality* and its eternal, infinite state of being. Once again, as soon as I understood this in the dream, a powerful feeling of sublime happiness overwhelmed me, and my awareness exploded like light in the night, enveloping everything. I immediately awoke. Again, it was so powerful and sudden, waves of shining energy surged through my body. There is no way I can come close to explaining the enormity of this feeling.

Although I felt myself getting closer to the meaning of my spiritual experiences, I was not sure if I should do something more with them. Were they provided for my own spiritual journey, of little relevance to anyone else? Why was I receiving this knowledge when many others were not?

As a novice in the monastery, I was sometimes called upon to serve meals to people who stayed in the guesthouse. On one such occasion I was approached by a woman in her late twenties who wanted to talk about spiritual direction. Due to my lack of experience, I phoned for one of the senior monks to come and meet with her. As we waited, she told me she had been searching for a long time for meaning in her life. She said she carried an emptiness within her that could not be satisfied by spouse, money or career. After many years, she came to identify this emptiness as a spiritual hole in her heart, and nothing could alleviate this feeling. That was why she came to the monastery. She was attractive and intelligent and seemed to have the world at her feet, and yet she was deeply unhappy. The senior monk arrived, she left, and I never saw her again.

I have thought about this person for over twenty years, many times feeling the sadness she carried at that time, as part of her day-to-day journey. She may not know it, but her role in this world had a deep and lasting impression on my life. Although I struggled with my own interpretation of spirituality, at least I'd had a spiritual experience to inspire my belief in a possible answer. Ever since hearing the desperation in her voice, I have searched for a response I could have given her, advice that might have given her assurance.

From the day after that first dream until now, I did my best to discover a way to bring that wonderful feeling of spiritual happiness into my everyday life. Foremost in my mind was the hope that it might have a positive effect on others as well. This book is for people who want to believe there is more to this life than the outer world of our senses. And there are many of you out there, because I see and talk to you every day.

If you think there is a possibility that a spiritual dimension exists, then this book is for you. If you do not believe this or are apathetic to the question, I would recommend, even for a short time, that you open to the possibility there is a place for you in this spiritual reality. The perspective of spirituality offered here might help you make some sense of our world.

The contemplations that follow are tools

for glimpsing that perfect happiness. What was revealed to me was purely spiritual, but my experiences were felt physically, with such power that all sensory awareness ceased. This proved to me that our perception of spiritual reality is just as relevant to the physical world as it is to the spiritual realm. It is a state of being and knowing that is attainable in this world, no matter what your situation or spiritual background. I hope the knowledge I share with you here will bring you into the sublime state I now enjoy. I have discovered it is possible to maintain this, even in the difficult world of our day-to-day lives. As time goes by and you notice the positive changes in your life, you will become confident the path you are following is right for you.

It is difficult to find the right words to describe the feelings and knowledge I received, to express these to you. You may feel there are other words that mean the same as what I've written but have more significance for you. For example, rather than *spiritual reality* you may prefer a word like Heaven, Nirvana or Elysium. If there is another word that evokes something deeper for you, I encourage you to use it. As you read each chapter, make these contemplations as personal as possible for yourself. Apply them to your understanding of the world. Picture how a spiritual frame of mind might impact your day-to-day life and relationships. Make this new perspective your own.

Each chapter begins with a concise contemplation followed by more expanded insights on its significance and impact. As you read and reflect on each of these, relate them to your own experience, identify the emotions that arise, and hold each feeling in your heart for as long as you can. Each contemplation has its right order, and the accumulated insights prepare you for the contemplations that follow. When you finish, feel these emotions as a whole, as if you were creating a super-emotion that encompasses all peace, love and joy. Try to do this every time you reflect on each contemplation, and in the final contemplation I will share with you what this super-emotion has become and what it means for you, for those nearest you, and for all creation.

PART ONE

PEACE

PRIORITY OF THE SPIRITUAL

There is a spiritual reality where spiritual beings reside. The spiritual beings remain in this realm; they have always been there and always will be. They have never left nor can they ever leave. I am one of these spiritual beings, and you are one of these spiritual beings. We are all spiritual beings, and we are all residing, right now, in the same spiritual reality.

The spiritual reality does exist, and it is yours to accept right now, if you so choose. It has embraced me, and, I hope, by reflecting on these contemplations, you too will experience this perfect realm that is yours and everyone's rightful state of being. This is a real alternative, and it is better than anything the material world can provide. The material world has very little to offer in the way of long-term happiness, and yet many people continue to focus on what little they are given, or not given.

It is not unusual to walk through society today and see people who are just existing, the weight of their unhappiness and anxiety holding them back from meaningful lives. Some of these people have given up on hope and are content to be lost. They choose to sit in the darkness, waiting for the time when their misery will end, expecting only to fall into nothingness. They ignore the personal happiness that exists just beyond – separated by a membrane that is no more a barrier than the decision to pull back a window curtain and look out for something better.

I want you to know there is more. Much more. By picking up this book, you have chosen to look through the window. And in making that decision, you will be rewarded with an opportunity to observe the same world from a different perspective. The truth is, whether we choose to do this now or at death, at some point in everyone's spiritual journey we all enter the spiritual reality. If we are willing to accept this possibility, why not anticipate what is coming and start planning? As everyone knows, half the fun of the celebration is looking forward to it.

In my introduction I shared three personal spiritual experiences. Although there are no words to accurately convey what I felt, I ask you, if it were you lying paralysed on the bed with your mind engulfed by shining light and energy, how would you respond? What sense of it would you make? I was not in another time or place; I was simply exposed to a different state of being, of awareness.

The world as I knew it did not have any significance in that state, and all I needed to reach this state were knowledge and belief.

Knowledge came through what I saw and felt: such as feeling the embrace of a spiritual being, such as watching people gather to accept peace, love and joy flowing from a well, such as seeing our true relationship with each other.

The second requirement was belief in this knowledge. I believed that what I saw was absolutely true. And what better way to know something beyond this world as a reality than to experience it in a dream?

When we dream, what our mind presents is what we see and feel. Since that first dream, believing in a spiritual reality was easy for me because I saw and felt its effect as real. And for this I will always be grateful. For those who have not had spiritual experiences, belief will be more difficult. Whatever the world throws at us, we tend to believe. We can try to imagine the spiritual in the world, but it is hard to see peace, love and joy when we are subjected to the opposite.

As we get older, belief in those opposite, negative feelings will damage our relationships, as well as our health and wellbeing. But the spiritual is truly here in the world, and, as you reflect on these contemplations, you will see glimpses of it everywhere. As you become more attuned to its presence, your doubts will diminish. It will be easy to accept the spiritual, and the spiritual reality will be revealed to you in all its glory, its light chasing all shadows from your path.

As you go through the contemplations,

certain ideas may strike a chord with you. Rather than learning something new, these contemplations may remind you of something you already know and have either forgotten or decided to ignore for whatever reason. When I was embraced by the spiritual being, I felt sublime relief as the feeling of energy subsided. But I didn't feel surprised by what I was going through; it was as though I were remembering what had always been, and this knowledge was such a relief.

Reflecting on this, I believe we already know what the spiritual reality is and who we are. The knowledge is deep within our being, and we just need reminding.

If you too have been fortunate enough to have your own experience of the spiritual, or if you have faith strong enough to accept the spiritual – either from what you have been taught or received as life-experience – then now is the time to take that knowledge to a higher level. Now is the time to decide, as often as possible, to turn your focus from the world and enter a place where spirit is all that is important. Rather than ignore whatever instruction you've received or whatever experience you've undergone in the past, use reflection as a tool to affirm the importance of spirit. Eventually, when you return to the world, you are seeing it from a higher vantage point, looking down on life moving around you, and maintaining that perspective as long as possible.

This contemplation and the others that follow will enlighten your mind to who and what is there, but first, prepare your mind to accept these truths. You need to be completely at rest for this to happen and recognise that the ways of the world will never bring you the lasting peace you need.

Throughout your life, you will enter periods of hardship and anxiety. At times, these problems might be intensified by your imagination, and, by letting go of them, even for a short time, you give your mind and body an opportunity to recover. When eventually you return to those everyday concerns, you are refreshed and stronger and better equipped to cope. Fortunately, with the benefit of hindsight, the older and wiser you become, the easier it is to see the cycle of good times and bad. Accepting that difficult times are a necessary opportunity to grow on your spiritual journey gives you strength to rise above your troubles, knowing they will pass so you can focus on things that truly matter.

So, for this first contemplation, let go of the concerns of the world, no matter how pressing matters may be. If it is just for twenty minutes at lunch, or in the afternoon after work, or in the middle of the night when you can't sleep, let the world look after itself for a while, and make a conscious decision to turn away from it.

If you have serious problems pressing on your mind, try to assign a time for worrying about them to a specific hour in the day. When that time comes, sit down and make proactive decisions on how to deal with those problems. But when that hour is up, postpone any more worrying to the same time tomorrow. What happens between now and then is to be kept clear of worries. Be strong about this. Treat all fears, anxieties and other negative thoughts like this. You have much more significant things to think about.

It is important you remain serious about

what your spiritual journey means for your being, and accept that absolutely nothing else matters. The spiritual aspect of your being is eternal and infinite. Relative to eternity, your time in the world is less than the blink of an eye. Relative to the infinite, it is as if you hold the world like a marble in your hands, as your mind perceives creation from the omnipresent spiritual. If you can keep this mind-set foremost in your day-to-day dealings, it helps bring weight to where your priorities truly lie.

Do you really have to focus on activities like entertainment so much? Must you spend your life worrying about how to gain more physical gratification? Do you have to work yourself to death for the sake of more material goods? You will never find peace with these motivations. I'm not saying you should give up everything and hide in a cave. I merely suggest that in each decision you make, keep your focus aligned on your spiritual needs, and ask yourself: is this pursuit important from the perspective of the eternal and infinite?

It is hard to turn from the world when there are problems like family issues or sickness and discomfort. But taking a serious orientation towards the spirit will be better in the long run for you, your family and all the world. You have to heal yourself before you can hope to heal others. In family situations, people in dark places don't need advice, what they really need is someone to share their pain. Someone who will sit with them and comfort them and remind them that they are the beloved people they have always been.

In the following contemplations you will learn how to do this, and why. Seeing others from this perspective will be more healing than anything else. Just try it, and let hindsight be the judge.

To make the spiritual your foremost priority, it is important to be proactive in searching for proof of the spirit. We live in an extraordinary age where we have access to so much information from all over the world. After decades of searching, I can tell you confidently the proofs are out there; all it takes is a commitment to look for them. They will be presented to you. Each time you believe you have found proof of the spiritual reality, reflect on its relevance to your life experience. Have there been past occasions where these truths were revealed to you?

It doesn't hurt to regard unfamiliar concepts of spirituality with a degree of scepticism, as long as you are not rejecting ideas because you don't understand them, or because you have been told to ignore them by others. Make up your own mind about what you accept. Only you can understand what is relevant for your spiritual journey; no one else can.

When you can successfully put the world's concerns aside, the first feeling of peace to explore is physical, a state of being suspended. It is as if gravity disappears, and you become weightless. Your muscles relax, tension across your body dissipates, and your mind frees itself from your body, as if jettisoned into space. There are many advanced meditation techniques that promote this, so find one that works best for you. The main point is to achieve that feeling of suspension from the world, including your own body. Your mind is all that is necessary when we pursue the spiritual. As far as you are concerned, time completely stops, the world freezes where you left it, and whatever meaning you thought it had becomes irrelevant.

As you reflect on this contemplation and the others that follow, try to perform them in a quiet place where there are few distractions. If it makes you drowsy or you fall asleep where you sit, fine. This means you are successfully allowing peace into your being. Just recommence your contemplation when you wake. As you progress, you will discover that surrounding noises or distractions have less effect. Eventually, the time will come when the world could be in complete chaos, and the quality of your contemplation will be unaffected. You are successfully prioritising the spiritual over the worldly.

PERFECT PLAN, PERFECT ROLE

There is a reason for everything you experience. All that happens around you, and throughout the whole universe, is designed for your spiritual development. Your perspective on the universe is unique to you, and that unique perspective was created for you. No one else experiences 'being' the way you experience it, and it is all happening as part of a perfect plan. You have a role of more importance for everyone's journey than anything that may be apparent in this world.

This perfect plan was designed for each of us to reach spiritual fulfilment. As you progress through these contemplations, you will have a better understanding of what that fulfilment is. Although the outer world plays only a small part in our journey to reach our full potential as perfect spiritual beings, it is nevertheless significant in giving us opportunities to advance. The more we embrace our spirituality, the more attuned we become to those opportunities as they present. During times of turmoil, we are pushed out of our comfort zone, and we experience opportunities to grow. When life is more settled and predictable, we have time for reflection and understanding.

Each of us has a role that we were performing long before we were born on this earth. That role has significance, not just for us, but for all spiritual beings. There is no such thing as failure or success in our roles; we were asked to perform these roles before we came into the world, and all of us agreed to do this. Some roles seem to be more attractive than others. Some roles are just plain terrible, and those people are subjected to the most miserable extremes. But, contrary to what we might think, it doesn't matter which role we accepted, they are all difficult. If an attractive person spends their life absorbed in their own beauty, they suffer rejection so much more deeply when their mirror reveals the inevitable degeneration of age. People who focus only on creating wealth will learn, sooner or later, that their attention should have been on their families and communities.

Throughout our lives we are subjected to influences that make us happy or sad or angry or bitter. The source of all feelings and emotions, whether positive or negative, can be traced back to love, or the lack of love. We are happiest when we share life with those we love. We are angry when people do not show love and choose not to treat us with respect. Our saddest periods of life are when love is taken from us; and we feel alone when times are tough and there is no one to love and support us.

As we get older, we learn to hold onto these feelings through memories and experiences, and this can either be very good for our health or very bad. We go through cycles in our moods. One day we're happy, the next day we might be sad, and there are times when we are at the mercy of our environment and circumstances. Generally, we have the strength to deal with daily problems as they come. It is when we allow past hurts to accumulate in our minds, holding onto them and projecting them into the future, with no desire to forgive and forget, that we find we cannot cope. Sometimes we have been so badly hurt that we hang onto negative feelings for decades. It could even be generations, if we convince our children to stifle their love too.

As far as our roles in this world, it can be difficult to see what special reason there is to endure these feelings and emotions, and how they could possibly help us achieve spiritual growth. The special reason is twofold. The first is to realise the depths we must endure to truly experience unconditional love; and the second is to learn empathy for others. If we reflect on past relationships that ended badly, we invariably find that our love for someone was subjected to a crisis, and we made a decision that because of the way that person behaved, we could no longer be with them.

Although we may not have realised it, we imposed conditions on the relationship, and if the other did not comply, then it was all over. True love does not have conditions. True love will never expect the other to behave a certain way. True love cares nothing for itself; its only desire is to love the other. I will go into more detail in a later contemplation that concerns the nature of the spirit, and this will also give you a greater insight into what the perfect plan means for us.

The second part of the reason we engage in our roles is to experience empathy, to understand and feel someone else's emotions as if they were our own. It is one thing to learn true love through our own experiences, but when we choose to learn through the experiences of others, our spiritual development in this world is super-charged. We do not just learn through relationships with family and friends, but with every person we contact. They are the people on the street, people in our travels, people from different cultures and socio-economic backgrounds, those we see in the media, those we read about in history, and those of younger generations who inherit the world we leave them.

Empathy gives us the ability to learn more about true love. It allows us to observe love from many more perspectives than we could achieve in just one lifetime of our own experiences. As we progress in our spiritual journey, we will potentially share in the love-experiences of millions of people. For anyone who has walked the backstreets of third world countries, we cannot help but be overwhelmed by the instances of love-expression around us. Yes, there is misery and poverty; and feeling empathy for the state of these people is a heart-breaking experience. But there are also community, commitment and rejoicing in these places, and this is also an important aspect of empathy.

To embrace the happiness and lovingness we see in others, with empathy, can provide a crucial insight into true love that may not be current in our own situation. Making it ours through empathy may provide the spiritual strength and support we desperately need at that time. By embracing empathy, we allow ourselves to engage in the larger community around us, and it is obvious what the positive outcomes will be if we choose to participate, both physically and spiritually. The sooner we learn empathy for the other, and for everyone, the higher we rise in our development as spiritual beings.

Everyone participates in this perfect plan, and the roles we play are unique to each and every one of us. But each unique role is interconnected with all others, and what one person does profoundly impacts those others. In some cases, a role might have significance for all the world and for generations to come. This doesn't mean however that one role is more important than another. Each and every role is extremely important in this perfect plan, and no role has a higher status than another.

Your emotions and behaviours are as significant to me as they are to you. It doesn't mean that negative behaviours are encouraged because these lead to negative consequences, and we don't wish that on anyone. It just means, at some point, you must experience humiliation as a necessary lesson in true love, and this can only be learned through the poor behaviours of others. You can choose to endure it, or you can step away. There is no right or wrong response, and either way you will learn.

How one person reacts to a situation may

be different to another's reaction, and, as far as the perfect plan goes, that is not your concern. Trying to discern what is ethically fair or unfair or why people behave in certain ways is, in most cases, a mystery. Even the professionals can't agree. You can only respond in the way your role has prepared you to, and, if you are thinking from the perspective of the spiritual, you can be sure that what you do is right. If you think you can help someone spiritually, you do, but there is no point in becoming upset if your help is ignored or rejected. They have their own perfect plan, designed specifically for them, and that must be respected.

Subconsciously your offer of assistance has been received, and it may only be a matter of time before this new knowledge is integrated. The next time you see them you may encounter a different person, for the better, and that is all you can hope for. Whatever their behaviour, learn to accept their role was designed not just to help them but to help you and others on your individual spiritual journeys.

The role you are assigned does not have to be part of the elaborate game you encounter in the material world. For example, it is obvious the motivations of many to acquire wealth at the expense of others goes against the nature of love and the spiritual reality. Of course, you need goods to make yourself secure and your family safe. But like everything that is not of the spirit, accumulating more than you need requires sacrificing loving relationships and is not healthy for yourself, your family, or those around you. Surrendering yourself to pursue your spiritual development will see these material priorities slip away from significance.

The perfect plan is not something you can redirect to fulfill your own wishes. You might have motivations that lead you in a certain direction, but if things do not go the way you want them to, it is because there is something more important you need to experience. To some degree it is correct that you work hard for what you believe is right for you. But if the situation becomes hopeless and what you wished to have happen fails, then instead of becoming unhappy, it is time to look for the alternative path that your spiritual journey is guiding you onto. Step out of your comfort zone and accept that whatever comes is for your own good. It is always one of the hardest lessons to learn, and it won't be last time you encounter these situations.

The older you get, the more helpful hindsight and reflection become for understanding how the difficult times of your life took you onto extraordinary paths you never expected to find. This is what the perfect plan promises you, and through reflection you will learn to trust the future will be more wonderful than anything you can conceive.

Learn to welcome all feelings, both positive and negative, from the perspective of true, perfect love. Share in the feelings of others, as well, and you will see your whole community flourish. Let go of everything with the realisation that in doing so you are allowing the best possible outcome for you personally and for others whose plans involve you. You can even look forward to all the potential outcomes possible, and here lies a deep peace that projects far into the future.

Learn to accept the world's only purpose is to lead you to a better understanding of your spiritual relationship. It is from this perspective you will affirm that the spiritual is vastly more important than the world, and this is the only road to lasting peace.

SPIRITUAL SUPPORT

In the spiritual reality there are guides who act as supports between the physical world and the spiritual realm. They are spirits who once journeyed in this world as you and I do. In that time, they realised a facet of spiritual perfection and are now an inspiring example for those participating in the world to follow. It is these spiritual leaders we turn to for guidance and support when our faith in the perfect plan falters.

As we strengthen in our belief that there is a perfect plan designed for our further development in the spiritual reality, there will nevertheless be times when life brings unforeseen lows, during which there seems to be little hope. Throughout our lives, relationships change, work circumstances take new directions, social circles dissipate to reform elsewhere. In the past when we struggled to deal with these changes, we found different ways to deal with it, e.g. alcohol, holidays, shopping. If we decide to make spiritual relationships primary in our lives, there will again be unexpected difficulties in pursuing this radical departure from what the world deems normal, but we soon recognise those crutches we used to lean on offer little to comfort us now.

Inevitably, by climbing further out of our comfort zones to pursue a spiritual destination, unobservable or obvious to others' senses, our social priorities will change from what they once were. How they change will be different from person to person, but if you decide you want more peace in your life, then perhaps you might choose a quieter path to walk that has less hustle and bustle. You may discover you don't always need to have so much social activity going on around you. You may find that certain people upset your inner peace, and you need more time away from their space. It can be challenging to let old influences fall away in this new stage of our life's journey.

Although your family and friends may be confused about the new direction your life is heading, most of them will welcome the peace you bring to your relationships. In the short term, however, there will be those who will not accept the changes you are going through, and it will be difficult to explain to them what you yourself are still trying to grasp. In fact, trying to explain might make them angry or hurt that you are choosing a different path over your friendship with them. It can be a time of confusion, and their frustration will only serve to make your life more difficult. More so when you are new to the spiritual journey, and your confidence and esteem are not yet strong enough to deal with criticisms and sarcasm. You cannot do this on your own.

As you surrender yourself to the perfect plan and relinquish control of worldly matters, the void is taken up by the unknown. Because you have allowed fears to govern most of your decisions in the past, it is easy for this void to become a place of anxiety, if you let it – particularly if your usual support groups are not as supportive as they once were. This can lead to feelings of loneliness and helplessness, and, combined with the daily pressures and problems of normal life, it is easy to be overwhelmed. This is when you turn to your spirit guide for help.

The spirit guide is a spirit that you choose, although it is more correct to say that the right guide is presented to you at the appropriate time. You might know the guide as a deity. The guide may have been a teacher in a particular religious perspective that you follow. The guide may be a person, relative or a friend who has passed away, but who you have always respected at a deeper level, i.e. both their spiritual awareness and how they applied it to the world in which they lived.

By the end of these contemplations, you will have a clearer idea of the qualities and values that will help you identify your personal spirit guide. You don't have to be concerned that you make the right choice; what you decide is part of the perfect plan, and your spirit guide is already prepared for your request.

It is important to note that the guide you engage with is a spiritual being who has participated in this world. They have endured the hardships here in this life that no one can escape. They have had to exist in difficult circumstances with their own fragile natures, like everyone else. But unlike the majority of people, they have recognised the importance of spiritual values and have done their best to maintain them; whether a leader on the world stage or a person confined to a household or workplace, whether they expressed these values verbally or through their actions. Their lives may have been cut short – we can readily see the spiritual perfection of a child – or they may have lived long fruitful lives in the community. In all cases, the guide has eventually left this world, and now resides completely in the spiritual reality.

The guide creates a bridge between the spiritual reality and the world you now inhabit. When you turn to them for help, they are aware of every thought, emotion and degree of unease you suffer. At the same time, everything involving your personal perfect plan is made clear to them. They know where you have been and where you are going, and thus they know exactly what sort of support is required. Their eagerness to help you is impossible to comprehend. There is no time lag when you ask for help. They are with you instantly, and, to their utmost ability, no request for support is ignored.

It is not their role to grant wishes or change your perfect plan. Whatever hardship you endure is for a specific purpose, to aid your development, and changing it would be detrimental. But sometimes a difficult situation is a catalyst for change, and you may be confused about your next step. Do you continue to remain in a difficult situation and see it as a sacrifice for something greater? Or do you pursue changes around you in light of where your spiritual path is leading you? These times are always hard to cope with, but they are the spirit guide's specialty. When you ask them for help in making the right decision, you can be assured that whatever you decide will be perfect.

There may be occasions when more than one guide is called upon at a time. You may be aware of spirits who worked together in the world to make it a better place, and it is their collective desire to help others who call for spiritual assistance on chosen paths. There will also be occasions when your life situation changes, and you might call on a different spirit whose experience in this world is relevant to your new situation. You need not feel that you are being disloyal to any spirit. They only desire what is best for you and your spiritual journey.

When there are conflicts in your relationships with friends, family and acquaintances, you may have tried everything you can to heal the situation, but nothing seems to work. Or you may see people you love spiralling into despair for one reason or another. You want so much to help, but you are either rejected or ignored, and insisting they change only makes matters worse. At times like these, you ask your spirit guide to support the spirit of the person for whom you are concerned, and immediately that support is given. Conflict will melt away. At times the change will be so sudden you will wonder if it is the same person you were dealing with before.

At other times the healing may not be so

sudden, and it will only be time that reveals the effects of the spirit guide's work. With hindsight, you will understand what support the spirit guide gave both you and your friend to heal the relationship and create an affinity you never thought possible. It is important to reflect on each time you ask for support, and its outcome, because it will give you more confidence in future, dealing with the different behaviours of people in your spiritual journey in this world. With confidence comes deep lasting peace, and in most cases, peace will heal relationships before they become a problem. Others will wonder why the office bully leaves you alone but targets everyone else. Why are strangers quick to help you when the world expects them to ignore you? You are walking with a spirit guide who will never leave your side, and is on hand to give you whatever is required.

It is the role of the spirit guide to support you in your hardships, and, as everyone knows, from a practical point of view, a difficult job is made easier when shared with another. Their direction gives you confidence you are saying the right thing at the right time, that you can speak your mind and stand up for yourself and for others, and that whatever happens you will have the skills to deal with it. All you have to do is ask. And you are encouraged to lean on them as often as possible, particularly as each time you do so, you reinforce your belief in the spiritual reality and the priority of spirit over this world. Each time you call on your spirit guide for help, this action brings you closer to the spiritual perfection they have already achieved.

Always keep in mind that your spirit guide is part of the perfect plan. The perfect plan recognises that you have reached a critical stage in your spiritual journey and that peace must be an integral part of your spiritual progression. In deciding to ask for help, you confirm that you want peace in your life, whether to recover from trauma, or to build strength for the next level to come, concerning your role. As you learn to trust in your spirit guide, your confidence in the perfect plan increases. Eventually you will ask for support less often and instead quietly rest in the knowledge that your guide is with you at all times, providing all you require, and ensuring everything that happens is perfect when seen from the spiritual perspective.

At all times, your spirit guide should be regarded as one of your closest friends. Conversation with them is easy because they only want to listen to you. If you could read their spirit mind, they would say "relax, everything will be fine, and things are going to get better. Much better." They offer you comfort and an intimacy you can never achieve here in this world. What they want for you, ultimately their most important role, is to shoulder your worries and provide you the peace and freedom to turn away from the world, as often as possible, so you can give all your focus and attention to the spiritual.

PART TWO

LOVE

OUR SPIRIT NATURE

Our spirit nature is the perfect expression of loveliness. Nothing can change or alter this. Your spirit, my spirit, the spirit of everything that exists, has existed, and will exist: we each share this fundamental essence. Our spirit nature only wants to love. It does not pursue any other desire, nor does it care if its love is returned. It was created only to love, and the recipient of this love is every other spirit in creation.

For countless generations, cultures from all corners of the globe have understood the importance love plays in our lives. The major religions of the world each have love as their core value. Our laws and constitutions have love for our ncighbours as their primary concern; companies and organisations base their mission statements on love. It is the mortar that holds the structure of our communities together.

Even though we recognise the significance of love in society, we constantly put up barriers within our relationships that block the flow of love, in spite of all history has taught us. There are many studies proving that deprivation of love causes illness, mental health issues and shorter life-spans. Children do not grow into healthy adults, adults struggle to cope in crisis, and communities fall hopelessly apart. It is not until we become exhausted with constructing barriers to love that we stop to look back at our past and recognise the possibilities we might have enjoyed.

So why are we required, in this world, to experience the opposite of love, often despite our best efforts or through no fault of our own? It is the question that is commonly presented as proof that spirituality is pointless. Why would a supreme being allow wars that destroy lives and cause so much misery? The answer is beyond our comprehension. However, we see many examples where people's response to a major disaster reveals the affection and love that lay dormant in a community until they had to strive together to rebuild their town. Before there might have been nothing but ignorance and indifference towards each other. For years afterwards, people express wonder at how quickly and efficiently their communities were restored to health.

When we commit to love and healing, and make these higher priorities in our lives, immediately our paths become brighter. It is easy to see the value of love in rebuilding a family or community, but it is during those periods of helplessness and unhappiness we endure – when we feel ourselves overwhelmed with despair – that we discover the true nature of our spirit.

Although it may be unpleasant to revisit times in your past where you almost gave up, it is important for your spiritual development to understand what happened or what is happening to you. Even more significantly, it is necessary you empathise with others in their misfortune, doing your best to imagine and feel their unhappiness as if it were your own.

The more opportunities you have to empathise with people in the world, the richer your spiritual development will be.

In the second contemplation, you explored the role of empathy. Learning about love is where it becomes most important. Just attempting to empathise dissolves inequality and heals. When you internalise others' experiences and connect to your own emotional response, you not only accept your equality with the other, you are better able to forgive any misconceptions you have had about that person. On another level, empathy allows you to learn about forms of suffering you may not yet have encountered in your own life. And why should you subject yourself to any more suffering than you need to? Through empathy with others, and through your direct experiences of suffering, spiritual reality guides you into the deepest depths of love.

Your spirit experiences your feelings and emotions as your mind does. Your mind and spirit are one being, and everything that happens to you is also experienced by your spirit. When the world-self suffers loneliness and rejection, the spirit suffers too. But the spirit responds to suffering from a different perspective. *Your spirit nature is the perfect expression of loveliness.* To express its deepest feelings of love for another, the spirit strives for the smallest, most insignificant position in the relationship. Any need for acceptance or demand for respect cannot exist, and that is why spirit will always accept the lowest place.

This is not something that spirit endures with frustration or impatience. Spirit welcomes selflessness for the sake of loving the other wholeheartedly. It sees the other as completely innocent of any wrong-doing. Spirit does not care about being hurt, nor about anything else. Absolutely nothing else. Your spirit only wants to love. This love comes from depths that we in the world cannot comprehend. Choose anyone in the world, and that person's spirit would suffer the deepest sadness for you; it would suffer the greatest humiliation for you; it would suffer infinite loneliness for you. This is where you recognise what your role in this world is teaching you. You are learning the deepest depths that true love will plunge to, through your own experience, and through the suffering of those around you.

True love doesn't mean we dwell forever on the pain of our past, or on the pain of others. We use this accumulated knowledge to understand that when the spirit loves another, it is willing to endure anything. Rather than feeling pity for people who are suffering, we feel respect and admiration for the difficult roles they perform – perhaps more difficult than anything we have faced ourselves. We recognise that though they may appear to be stronger than us, nevertheless they desperately need our support and encouragement. In the next contemplation I will discuss our relationships and why we take such an interest in others' roles.

Their roles are for your benefit. The spirit, yours and mine, would endure any role for another. It would suffer any darkness because it knows that only one thing matters, and that is love. Most of us have experienced love-sickness at some stage in our lives. Remember when you were so infatuated by another person that the rest of the world almost ceased to exist. You couldn't concentrate, you lost interest in food, you only wanted to think about that one person. When you didn't have the object of your desire with you, you shut yourself away and subjected yourself to waves of longing that were often crippling. You were in such a state of sickness; and yet you never wanted this feeling to end. You wanted it to last forever. It gave you an experience of true love, and revealed the sublime nature of spirit.

The spirit has no form or matter; it is only mind and emotion. Its beauty is not something we see but that we feel. The spirit's emotion generates energy that has no beginning or end, and therefore emanates throughout this universe, and beyond. Sometimes we can sense that transcendent energy in others. Though they may not be attractive in a worldly sense, there is something lovely and innocent about them that we cannot define but we know is special, so we want to be near them. As you journey along your spiritual path, you will become more attuned to recognising those individuals, and before long, you will see them walking beside you more and more often. It is because you too are generating this loveliness, and they are attracted to you.

The spirit nature observes everything

from a simple-minded perspective. If all that is important is love, then the rest of existence doesn't have to be that complicated. It also perceives that everything else in the spiritual reality is loving, and it will not accept anything less. It does not understand concepts like evil, ugliness, greed or hate. It could never conceive that other spirit minds would think of anything but love. Observing our environment like this requires an innocence that we have in childhood but lose when subjected to a world of hard knocks and negative experiences. Deep down we still recognise innocence as something beautiful, and it is a quality we must aspire to if we wish to get closer to the spirit.

It is one thing to accept the innocent nature of spirit, but is it possible to emulate this nature in our day-to-day, worldly lives? Unfortunately, we know there are people who may see innocence as special, but who also see it as a weakness to be exploited. Although we may experience conflict with these people, and at times be forced to react through fight or flight, we can still understand they fulfill a necessary role in our spiritual path. We may even recognise the development of a spiritual relationship that we share with this person. The more strongly we protect the purity of our innocence, the weaker the effect of negative influences on us. Strength comes from your belief that what you do is important, and that importance will be mirrored back to you when most of the world – those many individuals who don't want to take advantage of you – smile back with shining faces, reflecting the light of your innocence in their eyes.

During this contemplation, see your spirit as a being of pure loveliness. Spend time reflecting on what loveliness actually means. What qualities are expressions of true love, and when have you seen examples of these in your life? Have there been times when you recognized these qualities in yourself? Can you imagine walking through your day as a being of pure loveliness?

Learning true love is not an easy path. Putting yourself in a dark place to reflect on difficult periods of rejection and loneliness in your past – or what you see others going through – may not be the most pleasant pastime. Remember, though, that the spirit does not see darkness, it sees purity being unveiled. It recognises the strength, the depth, the resilience of true love revealed. It embraces this true love that is so deep, and which flows unimpeded through minds suspended in spiritual reality. All it takes is for you to con-template and realign yourself with your spirit. With as little effort as setting an intention, you can feel again the energy that shines through your spirit nature, which has flowed since the beginning of creation and will always continue.

OUR SPECIAL BONDS

Between you and me, between you and every person, between your spirit and every spirit in creation, there exists a bond. Although the bond may not be obvious in this world, in the spiritual reality it continues even now as strong and vibrant as the instant we were created. It manifests as a perfect union, each spirit absorbed in the other. This bond is a relationship, and the relationship between each pair of spirits is special and unique.

We were created with a special bond between each of us. It was not a physical thing, though it could be felt. It was a superior bond of love. It was part of our being that could not be separated or diminished. At that first instant, our love for each other was pure, pristine and powerful beyond words. There was an energy that held us together, an attraction of forces beyond measure so that our attention to each other could never be diverted. We were filled with overwhelming emotions of desire, admiration, and eternal loyalty to each other, and nowhere did there exist shadows of envy, possession or favouritism.

Nothing has changed between the spirits since that first expression of sublime intimacy. Those special bonds will remain as strong for all eternity – no matter what we might think of each other while in this world.

Each spirit is completely absorbed in another's for a special reason that is unlike any other relationship. Each individual carries a different facet of spirit that shines with a unique beauty, and all other spirits need this facet to complete their being. This uniqueness may be a form of strength, of grace or of divinity. It may have qualities that are way beyond our worldly comprehension. The uniqueness we possess is not something we hold with pride because we are more interested in the uniqueness of others. The uniqueness of the spirit itself is not what is important; it is the uniqueness of the bond one spirit creates with another that is significant. Each bond, although unique, is as wonderful as the next.

There is no bond that is greater or lesser than any other. No bond is more valuable than another. The bond you share with a beggar on the other side of the world is as important as the bonds you share with people living in your house. Although the roles we perform, during our time in this world, may have more significance for those near us in the short term, the underlying spiritual bonds we share should be our primary concern. We should never make the mistake of viewing the relationships in our worldly roles as being more important than our spiritual bonds. The worldly roles we perform enhance our appreciation of the beauty of our spiritual bonds – and that means of all of them, with everyone.

The bonds we share are serious. I need you, and you need me. If there were only one spirit bond missing, the love of the entire spiritual reality would not be complete; it could never be perfect. That is how special your bond is with the other. Realising its seriousness is an important aspect of performing your role in this world.

Sometimes we experience the consequences of ignoring this bond. The spirit learns more from such experiences because it realises just how great a gift these bonds are, and so it savours its relationships all the more. The alternative, that is, the possibility that there is no bond, would be unthinkable. When reflecting on the beauty of your special bond with another, hold close your awareness of this seriousness and recall it whenever you think of true love.

Two spirits can never be apart. Being apart is not something that can ever be contemplated. Awareness of this bond generates a transcendent love that no longer recognises there were ever two beings. Love is now the being, and not only is it infinite, it is eternal. There is nowhere and no time that your love starts or ends. It is everywhere and everything. That is the love between you, me, and everyone. There is no outside, nor are there outsiders. We no longer have to think like that. When you wake in the night, you are shining in the light of your union with all other beings. When your role takes you to dark places, you can remember your special bonds, which reassure you this time too will pass, and love will be rediscovered where it never left.

No longer do you have to be jealous of other worldly relationships that appear to be full of love and harmony when yours is not. They are engaging in a spiritual relationship to which you too belong. You share a special bond with all those people, and that harmony is something you too can enjoy. When you direct your thoughts to the special bond you have with another, and love fills your mind, all other spirits glow with appreciation at what they see. Their whole being is enhanced by your love, and waves of happiness flow out across the spiritual reality, to be appreciated by all. The power of each spirit bond is such that, when acknowledged, love increases exponentially into the infinite.

You are in relationships you don't have to work at. All you need do is acknowledge their existence. This spirit bond is greater than ties of family and kinship. It is far beyond what we look like to another, or how you might be of use to me. It is a relationship that never ceases to shine, each of us illuminated in distinct ways from each other. The brilliance this creates glitters with the light of a universe of suns, beyond anything you can imagine here in this world. Why would you ever want to leave this state? Why would you choose darkness over light?

It is the mind focused upon the world that chooses not to remain in this eternal relationship. Until you do, you will never reach the heights of happiness that are yours to enjoy. You can foster your spirit relationship in this world immediately. It only takes perspective. It does not mean you insist on now physically beginning your relationship with another, nor must you declare it vocally to the world. All that's required is for you to know it exists. A gesture as simple as a genuine smile to a stranger will reassure them of your shared eternal bond.

You share an intimacy with your enemies in this world that your spirit holds as dearly as the spiritual relationship you have with your closest friends. Although we all sometimes struggle to accept this truth, if you continue to follow the contemplations in this book and reflect on their relevance to your experience, slowly but surely, your knowledge and acceptance of these spiritual bonds will transform your worldly relationships in such wonderful ways as you cannot imagine.

You cannot experience the spirit in this world, either yours or theirs, if you do not recognise the special bonds you have with all things. If you allow negative emotions to control your thoughts, you place solid obstacles upon your spiritual path, which make it so much harder to traverse. Although eventually we all end up in the same place, you can choose a journey filled with happiness, or an arduous expedition filled with anger and anxiety.

Stop nursing hurts from the past; let go of brooding. If the pain is too hard to forgive, then try to forget it. If that is too hard then diminish the personal aspects and view the episode as a lesson you will never forget. And just move on. Let peace enter your life, and use your mind for nurturing the bonds and relationships you truly share because that is what your mind was designed for.

When you begin this contemplation, it will not be easy to accept a spirit bond when you cannot feel a physical bond. It is hard to believe that billions of people all over the world share a special bond with you, particularly when there is no direct contact with those others. For the spirit, distance means nothing. We could be realms apart and it wouldn't matter. Rather than using mobile phones or the internet to communicate, the medium we use to relate through our bonds is knowledge.

You already know what the spirit of someone in another country wants to communicate to you. They want to say they love you more than anything else; they would suffer any pain or humiliation or hurt for you; they will always be here for you. What more do you need to discuss? What more do you need to know about that person? You already know everything you need to know about the other, and that knowledge is more important than anything else going on in the world.

When we choose to acknowledge our special bonds with other spirits – and accept that wherever we are and whatever we do, they are with us – loneliness in this world becomes a thing of the past. Of course, we still need help from each other in the world, we still need physical support to perform our roles, but we never have to suffer the pain of believing we are completely alone in the world and that no one cares. Not only do we have our spirit guide by our side, but we have the loving support of all who reside in the spiritual reality, and we have that support forever.

CONSTANT LOVING FOCUS

The purest form of love is its expression. When a spirit truly expresses love for its lover, everything else moves to the periphery. In the spiritual reality, at no time is this focus of love anything less than absolute, and it is forever constant. The spirit loves with all its being, so selflessly, in fact, that its whole being consists only of its own unique expression of love. As its love becomes focused on the love expressed by all other spirits, it enters a state of being in-love. All spirits are suspended within this state of in-loveness, and here we reside for all eternity.

As you go about your day-to-day life in this world, there is something going on in the spiritual reality that involves you. Every second of the day, every spirit in existence is focused on you and expressing love to you. This expression comes from the depth of its being, and its being is completely immersed in that expression. If we, in the world, were to express love as our spirits do, our bodies would waste away; we would have no interest in food or entertainment or security; we would have no interest in anything worldly. This expression has no ulterior motives or agendas. It doesn't require a response or reward or any conditions. It doesn't care if it is accepted or rejected, and nothing can diminish the strength of its flow.

Although your mind is here in the world, your spirit resides in the spiritual reality and participates in this expression of love with all other spirits, whether you are aware of it or not. By a simple act of will, you can meld your worldly mind with your spirit mind, and once again participate in the union of spirits expressing love. Although the spirit loves unconditionally, for those living in the world, its pure expression of love is the hidden source of the beauty we crave. This includes feelings of being loved, of feeling lovable, of being in-love.

These feelings are what motivate us to live in community, to help each other, and to achieve great things for the sake of others.

To truly appreciate feelings of being loved, being lovable and being in-love, the lover and the loved must join in relationships where each learns what it is not to be loved, not to be lovable, and not to be in-love. There is nothing like a long fast to remind us how delicious food is. These feelings can be enjoyed without any kind of physical intimacy or contact. Just knowing there is a lover out there who loves us might be all that is needed to elicit waves of love, flowing through us and filling us with a heart-wrenching love-sickness. It is in our nature to desire these feelings, even when we continue to be hurt and exploited. Your drive to experience such feelings is the sole objective of your role in this world.

It doesn't matter who you are, your only purpose in this world is to deliver the conse-quences of being loved, or not being loved, back to the spiritual reality. These potent ex-periences of love enhance each spirit's pure expression. Every person who turns their mind to the spirit contributes to that expression through their worldly experiences. The spirits look with anticipation for the return of kindred spirits from worldly journeys for this reason: they will receive a new experience or perspective on the light and dark of true love, and across the realm there is much rejoicing. Every spirit's expression of love deepens and intensifies for having suffered, to the benefit of all spirits. Although it is difficult to imagine a spirit's love becoming any more beautiful, this is what happens whenever someone returns from the world to the spiritual reality.

Although feelings of being loved are important, it is the manifest expression of love that is paramount in spiritual relationships. This is what we in the world should aspire to when we reflect on the spiritual reality. When your focus is on loving all other spirits, your spiritual journey will look after itself. Your worldly role will also look after itself, as will your worldly relationships. This doesn't mean you shut yourself away from everyone.

When your focus is on the wellbeing of all other spirits, what needs to be said or done here in the world will happen perfectly. The perfect plan flows flawlessly when your focus is true. Learning to focus only on love takes time. There are many distractions to deal with, but each time you reflect on these contemplations, you will get better at putting distractions aside. It may be as simple as choosing the right place to sit to reflect or the right time to put down your smartphone. Your goal is to be able to focus on the spiritual reality anywhere, and at any time.

A tool of meditation is the affirmation. An affirmation is a practice of choosing a sentence or phrase that relates to your meditation and repeating it over and over. This practice helps you focus your mind on what you contemplate and leaves you less susceptible to distractions. It provides a rhythm to slow your breathing, which helps you achieve peace and wellbeing.

An affirmation is also the ideal tool for emulating spirit's perfect expression of love. If you use a sentence that declares your love for all in our spiritual reality, your mind is focussed and you can concentrate on the feelings you wish to convey to fellow spirits. The affirmation can be as simple as "I love you all, my beautiful friends." A sentence like this is saying all that needs to be said. Use whatever you feel comfortable with. The key is using words that express love to everyone. You will find after some practice that your affirmations become second nature for dealing with the distractions of the world, and they are an excellent coping tool in times of distress when you need help returning to a peaceful state.

Once you learn to deal with the distractions of the world, your next step is being able to focus your attention on all spirits at once. This requires an expansion of the mind to encompass all creation, and releasing personal incidents and betrayals of the past from your mind. Only in the spiritual reality are you able to engage with every other spirit at exactly the same time. You do not try to think of every single person at once; you rest in the assurance that every other spirit loves you exactly the same way, as they always have and always will. We are akin to the many spokes of a great wheel, and at its centre our spirit minds connect eternally.

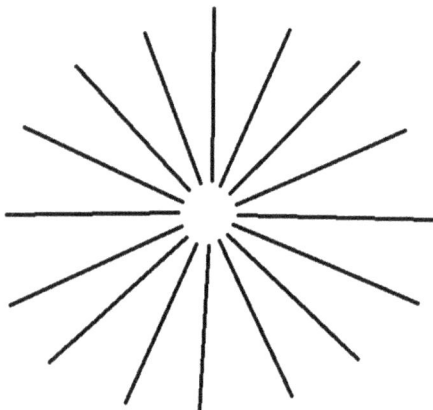

Each spoke represents each person's individual spiritual path, which has already been set out for them. The further we are from the central hub, the more distant we become from each other, and the more we feel lonely and believe our goals are different from others. As we journey closer to the centre, we become more attuned to our spirit mind, which resides at the end of the path. We also become aware of all other spirits and the paths they walk to reach the same destination. At the centre of this great wheel, there is a place of pure peace, and this is where each spirit's expression of love merges into all others.

This central area, surrounded by spirit minds completely focused on each other and the expression of pure love, is the spiritual reality. We bring with us our experiences of being loved, however good or bad, and our mind falls into this centre of perfect love. We are suspended at the centre of everyone's love, and what we experience is truly being in-love.

Our in-loveness holds us in this spiritual reality, as we join with all other spirit minds, both giving love and enjoying the feeling of being loved. We can either face each spirit and express our love and admiration through our special bond, or we can rest in the arms of countless spirits at once, thinking of nothing but loving contentment. This state of intimacy, of 'holding each other', is a gift our worldly roles have brought to the spiritual reality, revealing the strength of our shared love and our resilience, so that we never again let each other go.

The idea of the spiritual reality being a certain place is only metaphor. This realm of in-loveness is absolute and flows everywhere and through everything. All things are included, no things are left out, whether in the spiritual reality or in the world. As you walk in the world, you are not only acknowledging your relationship with all things, but you also reassure all things of their relationship with all else. Your mind is no longer self-focused but now thinks from the perspective of all spirits. You become the representative of all as you engage in relationships with others who are at different stages of their spiritual journey.

There will be times in this world when you are forced to relate to people who have no desire to unite with anyone, including you. We all associate with many institutions, every day, who do not share this perspective or understanding of the special bonds between us. This is life, and it makes our roles the challenge they are. However, nothing can alter the spirit relationships that flourish in your mind, and the contemplative state you cultivate cannot help but have an enormous impact on those around you. People will be attracted to your warm smile; they will watch with interest the way you resolve conflicts effortlessly with others. You will become healthier because your body becomes what it was designed to be… a vessel of loveliness, yearning to learn a deeper love through the art of relationship. Focusing on your constant expression of love for the other, in a state of in-loveness, is the only goal you need aspire to in this life.

PART THREE

JOY

RELATIONSHIP GRATITUDE

When we truly see the spirit of the other, when we know without doubt the love they have for us, and when we recognise the eternal, special bond that ensures we will never be apart, we are filled with unceasing gratitude for the relationships we share. Peace is the outcome when we receive True Knowledge. Love is the intangible force that binds us together with such strength, integral to our being from the instant we were created. Gratitude is the joy that intensifies our spirit relationships, and its light crosses dimensions to shine upon the people of this world.

To allow joy into our lives, we need gratitude. The most joyful moments in our lives reflect a transformation from 'not having' into 'having'. This applies to materialistic goods, to relationships, and to personal circumstances, whether health or security related. The state of 'not having' can feel like emptiness, but when we realise a state of 'having', the contrast brings about such transformation that we may never, ever forget the experience.

Holding onto that gratitude, right at the point you realise you have found what was missing, is a practice to maintain in all aspects of your life. Take delight in the small things you enjoy as well as the great moments you celebrate.

Forgetting to be joyful happens to everyone at some time. You can easily let problems consume you and tunnel vision obscure all else. It's possible to spend entire lifetimes focused on what you don't have or can't have or have lost. Again, this is an integral aspect of the spiritual journey because the gratitude you experience when at last you enter the spiritual reality provides joy for everyone who greets you there. However, there are some people who are willing to experience spiritual gratitude now, and who, in turn, make all our lives in this world more enjoyable. They are the ones who can show you how close the spiritual reality truly is.

For centuries, scholars have sought to understand the transformational experience of joy, often using the metaphor of travelling from darkness into light. They describe how it is as if an energy of excitement and exhilaration flows into people, changing their demeanour immediately, and they observe how quickly and easily darkness is forgotten.

When you find a way to erase darkness from your minds, you return to your natural state, and the light of joy once more becomes your normality. As you reflect on the following contemplations on joy, try to feel a sense of light and energy. The higher your level of joy, the greater your experience of energy... almost like a flowing power source that can be regulated as you wish.

To experience absolute joy, you must know gratitude at its source. You do not have to be very spiritually mature to realise there is little joy in pursuing material goods. All the money in the world means nothing if you don't have love in your life. In fact, it will only make the quality of your life poorer. Certainly, few of us enjoy living in poverty, but a poor community that supports its members has far greater health and security than individuals with only their material wealth to hold onto.

For a relationship to be healthy, you have gratitude for the other's love. Being loved is your natural spiritual state, and when you feel another's love, the truth of your lovable spirit nature is confirmed. This truth is often forgotten in the world, but when it is remembered, relief floods your being. Relief transforms into joy, and joy increases as gratitude is acknowledged and expressed. There is no greater gratitude than knowing you are loved for who you are. You are not being loved for what you look like, or what you have, or what you have done. This is the love of the spirit, and this is the love of all spirits.

Gratitude is the stairway that lifts the mind dwelling in the poignant depths of deepest love upward to the shining heights of joy. Watching the joy of friends, even of strangers, gives us much pleasure. It is why we give gifts on special occasions; it is why we volunteer our services to bring joy to the less fortunate. It is not only our own gratitude that brings us joy. We receive just as much if not more happiness when we see gratitude in the faces of those we love. Gratitude is such a spontaneous emotion, and our response to it is impulsive. We cannot help but be joyful, and love increases twofold. The more genuine their gratitude and the stronger its expression, the greater our love for them grows. Although this is a truth of the spiritual reality, we can see evidence of it in this world. In every culture and community, gift-giving has always played an important role in relationships.

Imagine your reaction when instead of seeing the joy they receive from a gift, you notice the joy they receive from your simple presence. This is where you enter the realm of the spirit. In spirit relationships, the gift itself means nothing. It is the motivation behind the gift-giving that is of prime concern to the spirit. This is what fills a spirit with joy. By sharing another's feelings through empathy, you experience their spirit's joy as if it were your own. You feel the joy they feel when they relate to you. You feel others' gratitude that you exist, and by 'others' I mean all creation.

Seeing and feeling another's joy is an exponential catalyst for taking joy to infinity. When I see the joy you have for me, my joy for your joy becomes visible and reflects upon your face, until we have a mirror-on-mirror effect that expands a million joy-reflections, like light shining out into the absolute. There becomes no distinction between the joy of one lover and the joy of another. This flows through all relationships with all spirits until there is nothing but our joy, and there is nowhere that is not our joy. This is what we experienced at creation, and this is what we remember when we return to the spiritual reality. We remember and realise that the flow of joy never abated, its energy never failed to shine through us. It is only because we were focused on other things that we chose not to see it.

This flow of joy is perceivable in the world we inhabit. If we catch the eye of another walking the street with the world heavy on their shoulders, it only takes a genuine smile to catch a twinkle of our reflection upon reflection of joy and gratitude. Our smiles grow wider, our postures straighten, and relationships are given an opportunity to develop. It is as if the flow had always been there between us, and all it needed was for someone to express it. They will catch on. Some days you might experience rejection through their self-absorption, or their confusion at the completely unexpected smile, but the next day you might see the same individual again with light shining in their eyes. Although they might continue to search for ulterior motives behind the relationship being re-ignited, the joy in their heart will certainly arouse their spirit, and then it is only a matter of time. Their spirit minds will be soaring.

Immeasurable delight is gained from reflecting on this. Strangers are no longer seen as strangers. You have a relationship with them before you even know who they are. The people in far off lands you have never met and may never meet in this world are at once a source of great happiness for you. You are no longer afraid to enter crowds because you fear what they think of you. You are no longer self-conscious about asking a complete stranger for help, knowing now that, in all probability, they will be only too willing to help you. Friends will discover a change in your demeanour; people will see something in you that is unusual in the world. You will no longer be perceived as a threat or someone with a hidden agenda. All others will see is someone who is completely comfortable with who they are, someone whose face lights up with joy in meeting. And, deep within, the hearts of all who come into contact with you will leap with gratitude.

Even with this wonderful knowledge, our worldly relationships will continue to test us. We are different people from different backgrounds with different codes of ethic. And yet deep down we all possess a yearning to get on together. To succeed in embracing gratitude starts with the decision to try, and then being prepared to find a way. Searching for reasons to feel gratitude requires effort, but even the act of searching elicits forgiveness and healing in our relationships. Gratitude requires humility. We must put ourselves in a position where we could potentially be taken advantage of, even if we have been hurt like this before. The truth is, for the few times we get hurt, it is worth the many, many times our gratitude will be appreciated. It takes courage to express gratitude and hope for the reassurance of another, as we form our relationships. That is what love is about. And the prize is joy.

Experiencing joy in this contemplation is the litmus test that your progress towards spiritual fulfilment is gaining momentum. Gratitude is the foundation for peace, love and joy; and when you accept this, you will gladly suffer any situation to express your gratefulness to others. Even though others in the world might not see a reason for your grateful joy, in their hearts they hope that your smile is for them and that, whatever may come, your face will always be there to remind them how important they are, even if the world seems to tell them otherwise.

GIFT OF GODNESS

When our roles are complete in this world, our consciuos minds will return to the spiritual reality where our true being has always existed. Thick curtains will be pulled from our sight, and we will see that all that is created is ours, as it always has been. We will recognise the splendour of Godness in every creature, every organism, every molecule, and we will know everything in the spiritual reality and its role in this perfect shining state. All spirits, both simple and complex, will greet us, and those billions upon billions of bonds we share, each as special as the next, will be engaged at once.

When we were created, we were given the gift of absolute spiritual being. There was nothing, in any realm, whether spiritual or physical, that was not part of our being. While we reside in this world, however, our roles introduce us to being apart from all else. We learn to appreciate the true depth of our love for each other and what we must endure to return to that state of wholeness within the spirit. Our bodies, and the concepts of space and distance, make it difficult to return to the perfect union of spirit, and therefore we look forward to the day true unity is achieved.

We have all experienced the anticipation of an upcoming glorious event, and we know this as exciting as the event itself. It is a perspective of joy we can take great pleasure in, particularly when the trials of this life wear us down. The stronger our faith becomes in the spiritual reality, the higher the intensity of anticipation we experience, and the longer we can remain in this state when we reflect on these contemplations. At first, we have to rely on our imagination to see what it is we return to in the spiritual reality, but as time progresses, the intellectual perception of what we anticipate will transform into emotion, doubt will be erased, and we will wonder how we could ever have forgotten.

You were given the gift of Godness at your creation, and although it is difficult to express the perfection and true extent of the gift you received, you can gain some understanding by focusing on three concepts of the gift in particular. They are All Belonging, All Knowledge, and All Engagement. These concepts are different perspectives on the same thing, and they can be known by one name or by all three.

The first concept is All Belonging. This means that all things that exist, have ever existed, and will ever exist belong to you. When you return to the spiritual reality, you will recall what it is to hold all creation as yours, never to be forgotten again. All Belonging means that you belong to everything else. You too will be held by all others, and your relationships will be renewed. All matter, space and time will be held in your hands, and you will see the light shining in all things as they were meant to be seen. You will understand your being is the light that shines out into all infinity.

The second concept is All Knowledge. When you return to the spiritual reality, you will know the reason for all that happens. You will know the perfect plan in which all have played a part and the significance of each of your roles. Your joy will be immense when you discover why you endured hardships in your earthly lives, and you will recognise what wonderful things you achieved on your spiritual journey for the benefit of all beings. You will never know doubt or indecision again, as all will be revealed. The future will no longer exist, and the past will be held as if it is this instant. You will know with perfect clarity that all that is important is your love for each other.

The third concept is All Engagement. When you enter the spiritual reality, you will receive the ability to engage with all beings at the same time. You will be able to express your love for each and every other spirit and to accept their expression of love in the same instant, and this relationship of perfect love will never end. It will be as if you are holding one person in a loving embrace when in that embrace you are holding all other beings. No one will be left outside that embrace. Imagine the joy that this all encompassing expression of love will generate throughout the spiritual reality.

Nothing in your spiritual relationships will be hidden; all beings will be observed in their perfect innocence as they were created.

These gifts were given to you without condition. No matter what paths you walk in your role on Earth, the spiritual reality and its gifts will be revealed when you reach the end of your journey here. You will see those you knew who arrived before you in all their glory, their faces shining as they see you reunited in spirit, never to be apart again. At that instant your mind will expand into infinity, into eternity, enveloping all that exists. There is no where you won't be; no thing that you won't be part of; you will be welcomed to absorb it all.

You will understand the significance of all you have learned in this world. If your role brought you into the darkest depths of fear and loneliness, the realisation of your true relationships will create a joy that is inexpressible. Relief will surge through you, then gratitude towards every spiritual being. There will no longer be any darkness. The light of your being will shine through all other beings and theirs through you. You will never tire of feeling the ecstasy of those spirits around you, as they hold you up with gratitude for providing them so much joy. You will never, ever forget this moment – the moment you anticipate in this contemplation.

Although we anticipate these gifts when we return to the spirit, there is no reason why we cannot enjoy the acceptance of these gifts as our own now. We already acknowledged all these gifts when we were created; only by participating in our world-roles did we forgot what we had.

Reflect on the idea that to possess physically in this world is not true ownership. You are withholding from your true being that which belongs to all other spirits. Reflect instead on sharing your enjoyment of all things in this world and beyond. Learn that you don't need to physically possess material things, but instead learn to enjoy what you see and take delight in others sharing these things too. Have pity for those whose roles encourage them to desire for themselves what isn't truly their own, for there will never be real happiness in their lives. Have compassion for those who spend their lives focused on the little rather than on the entirety of all that exists.

If you accept that peace, love and joy are all that is important, what other knowledge would you desire? If you can express love to everyone in this moment, and welcome the love of all spirits right now, what other communication is needed? You are already experiencing a taste of what is in store on your arrival into the spiritual reality. The deeper you can contemplate this imminent moment, and hold that knowing in all that you do, the sooner you realise the significance of all other worldly desires pales in comparison. All your life you tried to achieve a poor semblance of such peace, love and joy by gathering material things around you, and nothing ever satisfied your longing. All this time you sought in the wrong place and now, the realisation that you have found what you needed will bring you so much happiness.

That realisation gives you the strength to endure anything the world throws at you as you recall that hardships and sorrows are part of a plan designed for your benefit. You gain the courage to understand that everything that happens to you here, whether good or bad, is for your perfection and to be met with gratitude. You empathise with others' hardships and suffering, and if you are unable to help relieve their pain physically, then you express your peace, love and joy for them with all your heart. You call on your spirit guide to support those who are struggling on their spiritual journey.

If you can envision your own delight at what will come, look into the faces of those around you, and anticipate the potential joy for which they too are bound in their spiritual journey. Imagine their joy. See their faces light up with the wonders of the spiritual reality that will soon be theirs to experience again. Imagine understanding dawning in their minds as they realise what their roles on this world were for and how important they are for the spiritual enrichment of all creation. Although there may be confusion in their eyes, show them by the way you relate to them that you anticipate the day your true relationship will be revealed so your perfect, eternal friendship can resume.

Reflect on this shared anticipation, and in particular the instant of your homecoming. Imagine the contrast you will experience between your final moments on Earth and the first moments of your return to the spiritual reality. Imagine letting go of hardships and sickness to be embraced by the light of billions of spirits who welcome you with unbridled happiness.

Nowhere will there be darkness or doubt; nowhere will there be anything you do not know or cannot hold; nowhere will there be anything that isn't loving you. Anticipate your entry when all loving eyes will be upon you, at once congratulating you on the successful completion of your role in the world.

There will also be thanks because you contributed to the spiritual perfection of all beings. Anticipate the exaltation you will know as all spirits look with honour at the lessons you experienced and endured, and the insights you gained through others' roles. You will be revered by all, and all will thank you for doing what no one else could do exactly as you have done. And you will understand, at last, that everything you experienced in this world, absolutely everything, was worth it – a million times over.

REJOICING TOGETHERNESS

Sharing in each other's joy, together as a group, brings a heightened sense to our emotions. Sharing experiences together confirms truths, it affirms bonds, and it brings pleasure above and beyond what we could enjoy alone. For eternity we reside together in the peace, love and joy of all spirits, and we rejoice with all our being from the heights of the spiritual reality. Engaging in this rejoicing togetherness, we achieve the most perfect, most sublime, spiritual fulfilment.

All spirits, without exception, are in a relationship of peace, love and joy. This can never be changed, nor can it be lessened in any way. You were created as the perfect relationship, engaging with all others. From the instant your newly created spiritual being recognised itself, you realised you were being loved by all spiritual beings, that you were the cause of great joy to everyone, and that they were the greatest source of joy for you also. The only knowledge you had yet to learn were the depths of connection required to truly love in these relationships, and these cannot be known until you walk in this world.

When we enter this contemplation, we embrace each other's presence; everyone rejoices as we delight in each other's loveliness. We recognise the reason for our participation in roles and in everyone's spiritual journey, and we understand that whatever we endured in this world, or have yet to endure, is all worthwhile. We would go through it all again for the sake of our eternal relationships. Our challenging roles are easily forgotten when we focus on our spiritual path. Entering that place of spiritual togetherness, we perfectly express peace, love and joy *with* every other spirit. We immerse ourselves in an atmosphere created solely for our pleasure, and that is now enhanced in our experience of the world. This is what our spiritual journey brings us to.

Reflect on the realisation that all spirits are together sharing in the wholehearted knowing of everlasting peace, without doubt or anxiety, of being loved and being in-love, and the joy of gratitude. Not only are you enjoying your own fortune, but through engagement in spiritual empathy, you also experience the peace, love and joy of every other spirit as if it were your own. If you allow this knowledge to flow through you and around you, you can feel it as an energy of pure appreciation, building stronger and stronger within you to expand out into all infinity. There is no beginning or end to it, no borders or depth or height. And wherever it flows, you are.

You have always had the capacity to experience this togetherness, whether in this world or beyond, but for one reason or another, you forgot, became distracted, convinced or influenced otherwise. With this knowledge you never have to be unhappy fulfilling your earthly role again. Your role itself has become a source for rejoicing. Every person you meet, whether an old friend or a stranger, possesses a spirit who is rejoicing with yours right now, and singing wholeheartedly. There is a spiritual energy flowing between you that is stronger than anything produced in the physical universe, and it is impossible to weaken.

If you accept your worldly role is an important aspect of your spiritual journey, it follows that the world is, in fact, spirit as well. Although there appears to be separation between people, as spiritual beings there exists no barrier between you, no matter the time or distance. As you go about your daily life in this world, you carry with you the presence of all spirits from all possible realms. All beings are focused on your loveliness, as you are focused on theirs. All beings, through your togetherness, express a joy that radiates within and without. No one can deny the effect this will have in your world when you remember this truth.

You are together like one great family. But there are no elders or youngsters deserving more respect or less than others. There is no more respect for the intelligent or the wealthy than there is for the foolish or the poor. The outcasts of society hold as much importance as those who are attractive and popular. Everyone's level of rejoicing is the same, because you will realise that the people you rejected or ignored were truly your most wonderful friends. Rather than feeling guilt or remorse over your worldly behaviour towards another, you will rejoice at the highest level, as you anticipate your final perfect reunion.

No instant will pass by when you do not express gratitude with all your being for the blessed reunion of your true family. Your joy will be greater when you remember and empathise with those roles where you fell to your lowest ebb of unhappiness, in fear and loneliness – these were the dark depths your spirit endured for the sake of your lovers. The contrast you experience from dwelling in darkness to the shining light of true knowledge will be an extraordinary transformation, inspiring you to sing your gratitude and relief with every ounce of being. To remember this alongside other spirits who participated in your worldly lives, or who were nourished by your role, will perhaps be the greatest joy of all.

Realising the presence of all spirits within

this eternal moment, allows a deeper under-standing of your togetherness. You can feel another's spirit more closely than if it were a physical thing, and this closeness is accentu-ated by comprehending each spirits' complete focus of love upon the other. Every expression of love, every display of affection, is felt deep within you, in all its intensity and purity. No expression of love for the other is hidden or unseen. It will never be ignored or rejected. It will be received with open arms and held so close, and with such sacred solemnity, as never known in this world.

Together, we will also rejoice with wonder at the gifts we receive, referred to in the last contemplation. These limitless gifts of All Belonging, All Knowledge and All Engage-ment will never cease to fill us with wonder. We rejoice that all things belong to us and we belong to them. We rejoice that whatever knowledge we desire, it will be given to us. We rejoice that at any moment in eternity, we can communicate with whomever we wish, or with everyone at once if we wish. These gifts are a source of wonder that can never diminish, because they are infinite. They are gifts that never cease to continue being given to us. Our own joy in appreciating these gifts will only be exceeded when we see others' joy in accepting them, and, again, our shared experience will further intensify our happiness.

This perfect display of unity we express is the unfoldment of the Perfect Plan. When we arrive, we look back over our paths in this world and see how all its twists and turns were required to bring us here. For those of us still journeying in this world, we can stride forward with confidence, knowing where we are going and who is waiting for us at the end. The journey we are on can be enjoyed, and we anticipate, with gratitude, whatever else awaits us, because we now see the path with wiser eyes.

In togetherness, your purity of spirit is recognised. Forgiveness will no longer be necessary, neither for yourself nor for others. Feelings of guilt, remorse, anger and vengeance will disappear forever, and they will never obstruct your happiness again. You will see your innocence rediscovered in your spirit nature where it never left you, and it will be the foundation you stand on as you express admiration for the shining innocence you see rediscovered in everyone around you. Returning everything to its innocence is the catalyst for filling your world with peace, love and joy. It cannot be otherwise. To express your innocence in the world is all you are required to do.

Innocence is the key to experiencing true joy. When you rediscover your innocence, it is only your mind that needs convincing, no one else. You leave your past behind and embrace only the present. You let go of any darkness that you falsely believed was staining your being, and you focus on your lightness, suspended above all the ugliness you once thought part of you. As you gaze at the world around you, you allow others also to rise above their darkness. You have the power to do this. You have the power to create beauty where once there was none. Choosing to see innocence in all will elevate you enormously on your spiritual journey.

As we realise the joy in our togetherness, we feel our unified excitement grow into unbridled exhilaration. It is as if we no longer had control over our feelings, and our hearts are uplifted by an energy that has no name in this world. And yet it flows through all things, and is all things. The energy of this ecstasy rising in the hearts and minds of billions of spirits consumes the entirety of being. There is no beginning or end to who we become, and together we exist in a shining brilliance that extends through all realms.

FINAL CONTEMPLATION

GRACE AND REASSURANCE

The spiritual reality is a state of being where there can only be peace, love and joy; there is nothing else. Here we were created and united by our special bonds. Now we are perfected, yearning to feel each experience of heart-rending love ever endured. We reside in this state of evolving perfection, and we rest suspended in complete togetherness. In the vacuum we leave behind in the world, we see our new worldly roles revealed. The union of All Being, shining with the brilliance of supreme happiness, is now our identity and, as we walk in the world, we hold its perfection high for all to see. Keeping it pure from any taint, and projecting spiritual grace to all creation, we rejoice in our new role

*with confidence that all the world is now held
and reassured in our embrace.*

The previous nine contemplations opened
our eyes and hearts to the intense, positive
feelings experienced by spirits who are in
union with all others. Felt together, it is our
happiness at its most pure and perfect. It is all
light; there is no darkness. It is all energy; there
are no voids. When we reflect on this state,
our minds fill with the light of Godness, and
nothing can escape that brilliance.

All that was created is here, revealed in its
true form, nature, and purpose. We experience
a feeling that cannot be grasped or touched.
We perceive a state of being that cannot be
seen. But it is now more real than anything
that can be experienced in the world, and it
encompasses all dimensions, both worldly and
spiritual.

All creation is gathered here in loving togetherness, and all spirit beings recognise this
as their rightful spiritual home. They reside
here in the spiritual reality you have prepared
in your mind, and no one would ever wish
to leave. This spiritual home is where all are

comfortable, where everyone's nature can be enjoyed when desired, where the peace, love and joy of our perfection is normalised. Home is where we were created, along with everyone we hold dear, and where we develop and grow as spiritual beings. Home is where we spend eternity, knowing we never have to worry or be anxious again. Home is where we are being ourselves in all our glory.

When you experience all beings together, content in your spiritual home, you create an atmosphere that flows through you and around you. It flows through everyone and everything you come into contact with during the day. It is a joy that shines out from your being, more valuable than anything the material world might deem important. Although you might not sense it yet, this atmosphere radiates out much further than you can conceive. It enters all dimensions and realms, affecting all beings beyond this world, and beyond your immediate surroundings. You create an atmosphere of spiritual fulfilment that has more influence than you can possibly imagine.

By perceiving all you experience each day

in the light and warmth of this atmosphere, you engage with everyone, knowing your true relationship together. This engagement is total. Your mind focuses on all spirits as one, expressing your love for all others and your gratitude that you love who they are. Concepts like commitment, responsibility, trust, and faith are no longer necessary because there is nothing and nowhere else you want to be. You are doing what is in your nature to do. You can easily turn from the world and let its problems go whenever you want. You have broken free of the shackles in which the world kept you imprisoned and miserable.

Absorbed in this engagement with all spirits, you dive willingly into the deepest depths of expressing love you have ever received or given, by empathising with the journeys of others, past and present. You feel this expression of love emanating from the bottom of your heart – the pain, the grief, the gratitude, the joy – all those poignant emotions experienced on your journey to make you who you are. You admire the meekness and neediness of those around you who yearn for the loveliness you now project. Those periods of darkness they endured in their lives are now seen in their true light: as the most exquisite precious gems, which all crave as beings of love, and which reveal new facets of their loving nature that you could not have known otherwise. And you thank them.

Within this atmosphere of rejoicing, you enter a cycle of everyone loving everyone, and you rest in this loveliness of all beings. You may go for days where your focus is on loving the other, particularly if you have experienced a depth of love previously unrealised. You may see an innocence in somebody that you realise is inherent to the nature of every spirit, and you cannot bear the thought of leaving its wonderfulness for even a moment. You may recall the embrace of a long past relationship, realise its eternal significance as a sublime expression of perfect love, and see its purity shine out into all the universe and beyond. The cycle of love may then return you to rest in the lovingness of all things, content to flow in the enjoyment of God's gifts with all creation, as you were designed.

If you maintain this state throughout the day, expressing perfect peace, love and joy with all beings, suspended in an atmosphere of sublime happiness, you project a state of grace. The transformation of an organic mind into a generator of spiritual-reality dissolves all barriers. Infinity and eternity rush in to replace the space and time limitations by which you confined yourself in the world. This heavenly state of grace is all the world needs. The sooner you know this as your reality and experience it for yourself, the sooner you realise that nothing else matters and there is no world-agenda that cannot be ignored. See that what happens around you is designed to take you away from the world of selfishness and despair. See that this perfect plan is guiding you instead to supreme happiness.

Your new role is to walk in the world offering the grace of spiritual togetherness to all who need it. And everyone needs it, no matter what they might think. Whatever skills you possess or position you hold will be enhanced by the knowing you now carry with you, day after day. The spiritual reality is everyone's perfect happiness expressed as one. It is expressed as one, it is felt as one, and it is seen as one.

See your friends about you being consumed by this happiness. In your mind's eye, see it transform their faces, see them cry out with joy and relief that this happiness is their true identity. Recall the strangers you may have met recently. See them filled with the same shining happiness. As you gain confidence in your new role, see those with whom you are not so friendly also transformed by peace, love and joy. In doing so, you ensure that no one is excluded from the spiritual reality you hold, because, if even one being is excluded, this perfect realm cannot exist. You will discover you have the strength and the spiritual support to make this possible. All you require is the desire to be your true self, and to see them as they truly are.

When you dwell in your spiritual home, and when you allow absolutely everyone entry to this shining reality of purity and perfection, it is time to envelop the world with your beautiful mind. In the beginning this might be easier said than done. Although I have had the good fortune of knowing these truths for years, and I have seen the wonders this knowledge produced in the world around me, there are still times when I experience difficulty maintaining this state of perfection through the ups and downs of my spiritual journey. But each time I am challenged I learn something new, and the sooner I return to the comfort of my eternal relationships, the sooner my perspective is repaired and I am ready, once more, to embrace the world through this vision of our loveliness. The shining splendour of the spiritual reality is now your mind, and its light is only as fragile as your thoughts and intentions allow it to be.

The spiritual reality is no longer a place that is distant and remote. You have allowed your mind to be a glorious eternity, and it radiates through you with an atmosphere not of this world. You bring your vision of spiritual perfection to the here and now. To maintain this state of pure, innocent love, you keep your mind clear of negative thoughts. You take great care not to taint what you now know is wonderful. It is easy to understand how worldly pursuits such as greed, lust and envy are detrimental to your ability to keep everyone close to you in spirit. You examine your daily motivations and plans in the light of your spiritual relationship so that any flaws are revealed and can be avoided. In the spiritual reality, there is no doubt about what is right or wrong.

Your role leads you into a new dimension, and the spiritual path you follow becomes straighter, with less deviations. Projecting the spiritual reality will have a deeper and more lasting effect on the world than you might immediately perceive. Your mind becomes a place of affirmation and rejoicing, and the spiritual reassurance this generates now shines upon everything in the world and beyond, both physical and spiritual. When you feel you have lost direction in life or need motivation to focus on your eternal relationships, seek to give gentle reassurance to others who are lost in the world, for as long as you can. The spiritual reality will forever sing with gratitude for the new role you have accepted and with which you are now engaged.

As the intimacy of your spirit relationship deepens within you, the empathy you feel for people around you will express itself as sympathy and compassion. There is not a person in this world who does not deserve our sympathy: the young and fearful, the attractive and insecure, the wealthy and lonely, and the elderly and infirm. Their roles inspire you to nurture them with deepest compassion for their situation, particularly when you recognise that what they endure is all for the sake of love. Anticipating their eventual realisation of your spiritual relationship brings you much happiness, and realising your true connection with these people brings a light to your eyes, which they will see as a mirror for the shining light of their own spirit knowledge, hidden deep in the subconscious of their world-focused minds.

The further you are from knowing your true spirit relationships, the more desperate your need for reassurance. It is necessary for all to experience this neediness at some time, for it enables you to enter depths of love that can only be felt and comprehended through experience. A significant aspect of your new role is to offer help, kindness and support whenever possible to those who suffer from loneliness and rejection. Letting everyone know you are one who offers comfort will allow others to express their neediness. This will be a great benefit to their spiritual growth, and to yours. From your spirits' point of view, seeking reassurance is a source of humility it would gladly suffer for all eternity, such is the extent of its love for all others.

As you offer grace and reassurance, in your new role, it is important to understand that you are not trying to control people around you. You do not want people to behave a certain way in response to the atmosphere you project, nor do you insist the circumstances around you should change. It would be nice if conflict in the workplace ceased or harmony returned to your community. However, you are confident, with the influence of a spirit mind, that whatever is happening in the world now is part of the perfect plan. Your only desire is for others to catch a glimpse of your eternal relationship, even if they have no comprehension what they are seeing. You feel reassured they are being nurtured at a spiritual level, and that is all they need.

Introducing this spiritual reality into the world has enormous consequences. A loving interaction with one individual creates a ripple effect that extends outwards to all people around you, both spiritually and physically. At times there may be barely a sign that anything has taken place, but it has. As your faith in this process increases, and your powers of hindsight and reflection become more attuned, you will see this more clearly. You will no longer hope for miracles or blessings because acceptance will imbue your everyday experience with grace. These things are not being made to happen; they occur because you provide the conditions for peace, love and joy to exist. The perfect plan will do the rest.

CONCLUSION

Dare to dream of perfect happiness on Earth, forever enjoying everyone's loveliness and perfection. Strive to make it a reality in your day-to-day life. This is now your new role in the world, and all that you need will be provided.

It doesn't matter who we are, worldly life brings hardships upon us. I now work as a pastoral carer in a hospital, and it is heart-crushing to see the despair so many people endure on a day-to-day basis. Rose-coloured glasses don't work here. However, you don't need glasses to see how grace flows as compassion through the relationships of people who provide and receive medical care. We all experience illness and crisis at some stage in our lives, but we also experience the grace that threads through it. At our lowest points we are most appreciative of the beauty of grace. When we recognise its beauty, and reflect upon it, we also appreciate its utmost importance for our spiritual growth.

By engaging in these ten contemplations to enhance your spiritual understanding, and by holding close the comfort of your eternal relationship with all that exists, you will glide effortlessly through the worst that life throws at you. Hardships depart as quickly as they arrive, and, once more, peace, love and joy return to their rightful place in your heart and mind. Over time these contemplations will become the foundation upon which all your worldly relationships develop. Remember, there is absolutely nothing more important than your relationship with a fellow spirit. Everything you do in this world, have done and will ever do, leads to this. The sooner you grasp the significance of this truth, the sooner you will experience life the way it should be: in harmony with all.

How unsettled your existence is now, and how motivated you are to meet the challenges of transformation, will govern how long it takes to return to the perfect being you really are. Transformation is never easy. However, when your nights are filled with dreams of reunion and intimacy, you will know you have made the right choice. When you realise with hindsight that everything you needed was provided for your journey, conviction will be your response to new challenges. I have attempted to articulate what enjoying our eternal relationship will mean for you, but ultimately you need to experience it for yourself.

To strive for deeper intimacy in your relationship with each and every spiritual being, you will want more time and space where you are not distracted. As time goes by, you will rid yourself of distractions so you can plunge deeper into the loving, emotional support you enjoy within, the sublime spiritual reality that fills your mind. You will be grateful to wake in the night when all is quiet, and this time for engaging with all spirit beings is your own. It doesn't matter when and where you open your mind to them, those joyful lovers who would endure anything for you are there, waiting with anticipation for your attention.

Take your time with the contemplations. As in any new discipline, following a routine will make discernment of your spiritual progress less daunting. Discover the truths that these reflections contain for illuminating your own experiences and beliefs, and personalise the practice as needed. At first some contemplations may resonate more deeply with you than others, but eventually you will discover they all complement each other. Whenever possible, set time aside so each contemplation can be reflected upon through the day. There may be longer periods when you are unhappy or feeling down, and you might want to focus only on returning to that higher state of joyful thoughts. If it lifts your heart, then certainly embrace that joy. But it is important you don't neglect the other contemplations of love and peace. Over time you will understand why they are all necessary.

How I arrived at the concepts in these contemplations may, at first, not be obvious from the spiritual experiences related in my introduction. I have interpreted my spiritual experiences and their significance in relation to my own role, and I hope my insights will be relevant to you. I want to reassure you that, after years of reflection, these contemplations continue to connect me to the reality of our spirit relationships, which I was fortunate enough to realise in my initial experiences. Embracing these contemplations has enlightened me to a pristine experience of the spirit more powerful and more glorious than I could once have comprehended.

These contemplations evoke feelings, and, once you are able to commit each reflection to memory, I hope you will memorise those feelings in your heart. It will be as if you gently pour these feelings together so they are absorbed, as if into one. What you will absorb are ingredients for the perfect happiness that is your true spiritual state. When you attain that spiritual state and can hold it easily in your mind, next envision the same shining happiness for every other being, and let this replace everything you thought you were. Let all intellects, both yours and theirs, be focused only on our rejoicing togetherness. Offering up your mind as a home for all spirits, so deeply in-love, will allow something shining with splendour into the here and now. You will create a place in the world for the spiritual reality where before there was none.

Although you may never be aware of the impact of your path on others, the spiritual support you generate will circulate throughout the whole world. It will be a stimulus for the spiritual leaps and bounds everyone takes as we recognise the breadth of peace, the depth of love, and the height of joy that are mostly hidden in this world. These realisations will replace doubt with truth, resignation with hope, and shine a guiding light on others' spiritual paths. When you let go of your perceived differences, these gifts are for everyone's enjoyment. Make a decision to embrace the togetherness of all spirits, to love forever all those who truly want only to love you, and to delight in the special bonds you share for all eternity. Enter the splendour of a spiritual reality that is all around you, be with your friends, and let whatever happens in the world be the perfection it is meant to be.

www.ingramcontent.com/pod-product-compliance
Lightning Source LLC
Chambersburg PA
CBHW052109090426
42741CB00009B/1736